T0131928

MY SEOUL

(SOUTH KOREA)
LOCAL BUDDHIST TEMPLES

PHOTOGRAPH MEMOIR

DANIEL NARDINI

To order additional copies of this book, contact:
Xlibris
844-714-8691
www.Xlibris.com
Orders@Xlibris.com

ISBN: Softcover   979-8-3694-0992-3
               EBook   979-8-3694-0993-0

Print information available on the last page

Rev. date: 10/19/2023

Contents

Dedication

I dedicate this book to my dearest friend Wang Sih Cheng (whom I respectfully called Mr. Wang). Being a devote Buddhist during his lifetime, we met at one of the local Buddhist temples, Bongwonsa, and along with many things we always had that place to remember. I dedicate this book to my beloved wife Jade Nardini (maiden name Ryu Hwa Soon) who has been my faithful companion for all these years. I wish to dedicate this book to my manager for Lawndale News Pilar Merino Dazzo for her help and for all of the years we have worked for the newspaper together. I also dedicate this book to the Sterling Public Library in Sterling, Illinois, for their help in making this book possible.

The Beauty of Seoul's Buddhist Temples

I lived in Seoul, Republic of Korea (South Korea), from February of 1996 to March of 1997. I worked as a foreign English teacher for English Language School International (ELSI) in Korea, teaching adults. Some of the places that attracted me from the beginning when I lived in Seoul were its Buddhist temples. I lived in the city district called Seodaemun, and not far from my apartment was the Buddhist temple complex known as Bongwonsa. I used to walk there all year-round and stay there for a few hours to look around. This was one of the local Buddhist temples in Seoul, and one of the most famous. It was at this temple complex that I met my dear friend Mr. Wang who would become one of my best friends in South Korea and one of my best friends in life.

Mr. Wang and I shared many memories of meeting at Bongwonsa. I saw Mr. Wang pray to Lord Buddha at one of the shrines, and even make an offering. He knew some of the priests at the temple complex, and at his home he had a small statue of Lord Buddha. He taught me many things about both Buddhism as well as something about Taoism since that was part of his Chinese cultural heritage (he was an ethnic Chinese born in Korea of ethnic Chinese parents who settled in Korea from Shandong province in China). Because of his Buddhist faith, he connected with so many Koreans, and he participated in many rituals as well as celebrations like Buddha's Birthday.

He also introduced me to the Buddhist temple complex in central Seoul known as Jogyesa. For Mr. Wang, the Buddhist faith did not matter if it was Korean or Chinese. The faith surpassed any and all borders and all nationalities. Like Bongwonsa, Jogyesa has a long history. My girlfriend and soon to be wife Ryu Hwa Soon (Jade Nardini) introduced me to yet another famous Buddhist temple complex known as Bongeunsa. These three Buddhist temple complexes are visited by hundreds of thousands of devoted Korean Buddhists every year. These places have played an important part in my life when I lived in Seoul, When I returned from time to time to visit Seoul from 1998 to 2007, I frequently visited these important local Buddhist places of worship.

Daniel Nardini
Chadwick, Illinois
2023

Bongwonsa

During my days off from teaching, I walked across Ahn Mountain to the other side to the Buddhist temple complex Bongwonsa. I did this every single month, regardless of whether it was summer or winter, and for sheer relaxation or to visit my close friend Mr. Wang. As I sat on the ledge of one of the platforms of a main temple hallway, I gazed at the other temples and shrines where a beautiful golden Buddha statue sat as worshipers went from place to place paying their respects to Lord Buddha. My friend Mr. Wang did the same. I greatly admired the beautifully wooden carved roof beams, the intricately hand-painted murals on the walls, the elegant wooden doors that led into the temples, and the large array of golden Buddha statues each on a fine pedestal.

The history of Bongwonsa (sa meaning "temple") is shrouded in history. The temple was said to have been founded in the year 889 CE (Current Era) by the Korean Buddhist monk Doseon during the Silla Kingdom from 57 BCE (Before the Current Era) to 935 CE. The temple complex existed in the area that would later become the capital Hanyang (modern Seoul) of the Joseon Kingdom (1392 to 1897). In the 18th Century, Bongwonsa was moved to its present location on Ahn Mountain; its previous location later becoming Yonsei University in the 19th Century.. This is why the oldest temples in Bongwonsa are no older than 250 years old. Why are there no older ones surviving? Part of the answer are the wars that had been occurring on the Korean peninsula. Another hazard was fire. Because the temples were mostly made of wood, they easily burned down. During the Korean War alone (1950 to 1953), parts of Bongwonsa were damaged, but the temple complex largely escaped complete destruction.

What makes Bongwonsa different from most other temple orders is that it is the headquarters of the Taego Order of Korean Buddhism. This allows its priests to marry (although not its monks or nuns). Like all Buddhist orders in South Korea, it is part of the Mahayana sect of Buddhism as is true in China, Japan and Vietnam. When I reached the temple complex I would drink the mountain water that came from Ahn Mountain, and I would wash my hands as is custom there. Festivals were held there, including probably the largest one for fervent Buddhists known as Buddha's Birthday (I will say more about this one later). While many of my teaching co-workers headed to the bars, I went in search of peace and quiet as well as spiritual fulfillment at Bongwonsa.

Bongwonsa Photographs

The road leading to Bongwonsa

The leading prayer hall

A statue of Buddha in the prayer hall

A reception hall for the monks, nuns and clergy

Statues of Buddha and boddhisatvas

Statues of Buddha and his original disciples (left). To the right
are photographs of deceased Buddhist followers

A shrine on the grounds of Bongwonsa

Statue of Buddha in the shrine

Faded centuries old paintings of the east and west guardians (famous guardians in the Buddhist faith protecting the Lord Buddha) on the gates leading to Bongwonsa

Joseon-era palanquin used to transport a statue of the Buddha to its altar in the temple

Jogyesa

While I took a break between teaching classes, I went to a well-known Buddhist temple called Jogyesa. Right next to the historic street known as Insadong in downtown Seoul, Jogyesa is frequented by many Buddhist adherents going to the main temple to pray, offer donations, and wander the temple grounds. Jogyesa is close to the largest of the royal palaces Gyeongbokgung. I went to this place to admire the temple and those historic buildings on its grounds. There are also two trees that have by themselves become historic cultural assets. They are the Chinese Scholar tree and the White Pine tree. They were brought to this temple 500 years ago by Chinese Buddhist missionaries. Despite the inadequate soil and the limited space on the temple grounds, these trees have survived not only the soil but Korea's turbulent history to the present day. Indeed, Jogyesa itself has survived Korea's turbulent history.

Jogyesa was founded at the beginning of the Joseon Kingdom in 1395 CE. The main temple was said to have been constructed in 1395, and the temple complex survived war and invasion. Strangely enough, Jogyesa survived the Japanese invasion of Korea from 1592 to 1598, despite the Japanese having burnt down most of Hanyang (now called Seoul) to the ground. In the early 20th Century the Japanese returned and made Korea a Japanese colony. No, this did not go down well with the Koreans and especially Korean Buddhists as well as Korean Christians. Interestingly enough, Jogyesa became a focal point of resistance to Japanese colonial rule, and many Korean Buddhists found themselves in Japanese prisons. After Japan lost World War II, and when the Republic of Korea was founded in 1948, there was a strong Buddhist revival in South Korea which continues to this day.

Jogyesa is the headquarters of the Jogye Order of Son (called Jian in China and Zen in Japan) Buddhism, which practices celibacy for all in the order. The Jogye Order has many Buddhist temples throughout South Korea. This has been true for centuries. One other thing that I found interesting is that the street lining the way to the temple has a lot of Buddhist shops selling everything from Buddha statues to clothes for monks, priests, nuns, and miscellaneous such as prayer beads, holy water, water fountains with Buddhist designs, vegetarian food, candlesticks, altars for putting up Buddha statues, beautiful scrolls with calligraphy in both classical Chinese and Korean hanguel (Korean alphabet) with sayings from the Buddha, and Buddhist textbooks. Anything that a Buddhist adherent could possibly want for becoming a part of the Buddhist clergy or just learning more about Buddhism can be found in all of these specialty shops near Jogyesa.

Jogyesa Photographs

Jogyesa temple grounds. The entrance gate is right behind

The main temple at Jogyesa

The entrance side to the main temple

The beautiful intricate artwork in the wooden Panels

The panel artswork reveals the story of the Buddha

Because of the age of the building, a metal beam is holding up part of the roof.

The old belfry where the bell was rung for the change in the routine of the monastery

An old stone lantern that had been used for lighting ages ago

Part of the Scholar Tree on the temple grounds. Note the stone fence surrounding it

The pine tree on the temple grounds that had been brought by Chinese Buddhist missionaries 500 years ago

Bongeunsa

I did not even know about this Buddhist temple complex until my girlfriend (now my wife Jade Nardini) took me there. Located in the southern area of Seoul near the rich district of Gangnam, Bongeunsa was founded in 794 CE during the Silla Kingdom (629 to 950 CE). When the Joseon Kingdom was established in 1392, Bongeunsa was reconstructed under the patronage of Queen Jeonghyeon in dedication to her husband Seongjong. During the Middle Joseon period, Bongeunsa served as the Buddhist national examination center for Buddhist priests from 1552 to 1564.

When the Korean Empire was established from 1897 to 1910, Bongeunsa became recognized as one of the most prominent Buddhist temples in the country. In 1939, many of the buildings of the Bongeunsa temple complex were destroyed by fire. Like almost all of the temples in Korea being made of wood, fire was a common hazard. In 1950, almost all of the temple complex that had survived the fire were destroyed or damaged in the Korean War. Despite the destruction Bongeunsa had suffered, one of the temple main halls called Panjeon had escaped destruction and remains largely as it originally was when it was built during the Joseon Kingdom. Panjeon is notable for housing the wooden printing blocks for the Flower Garland Sutra created by the famous monk Yeonggi.

Today, Bongeunsa is visited by Buddhist clergy from all around Korea as well as the Buddhist faithful from around the country and tourists. I found the architecture magnificent. Bongeunsa is impressive for all who want to learn something about Korean Buddhism. It is also a nice escape from the urban landscape of Seoul.

Bongeunsa Photographs

The main entrance to Bongeunsa

Door painting of the East Guardian

Door painting of the West Guardian

Statues of the East and West guardians at the inner entrance

The main temple in Bongeunsa

Monk's quarters in Bongeunsa

One of the worship halls (photo 1)

A closer view of the worship hall (photo 2)

A shrine on the temple grounds

Another shrine on the temple grounds

The author's fiancé next to a shrine

Buddha's Birthday

Held in either April or May (depending on what week it falls on in the Korean Lunar Calendar), Buddha's Birthday is a major celebration for the Buddhist clergy as well as the faithful. I had never seen anything like it before I lived in South Korea. Just a week before the celebration began, colorful paper lanterns were strung up from one end of the temple buildings to the next. The whole grounds were covered by these paper lanterns for the next ten days (most of the paper lanterns were red, yellow, green, and orange or a combination of all of the above. Bright colors symbolizing a happy occasion). At night, the monks turned on the lanterns so they lit up the temple area; the paper lanterns having little electric lights in them. The monks and nuns would hold concerts playing on traditional Korean instruments for the Buddhist faithful or non-Buddhist visitors.

During the ten days of Buddha's Birthday, huge tapestries of the Buddha as well as other Buddhist deities would be displayed outside of the temples. These tapestries were made probably centuries ago of the finest cloth and painted by the finest artisans of the period. The faithful would pray to these images of the Buddha as well as make offerings. Incense would be burned outside and the faithful would fill the temple halls to give prayers to Lord Buddha. As more of the faithful came to the temples, they would drink the mountain water and wash their hands in a ceremony of purification. The monks and nuns would prepare vegetarian food for those who came to the temples, and the faithful would put money into donation boxes left throughout the temple complexes. It was not uncommon for priests, monks and nuns to come from other Buddhist temples for visits and stay for a night or two.

During the daytime, I observed the faithful, and especially elderly people, enjoying themselves. People might take part in traditional Korean dance, elderly men might play a traditional game called paeduk (similar to the game "go" in Japan where the objective of the game is to get five pieces in a row), and whole families got together to have picnics. At the time, this was a festival that was not commercialized or turned into an enterprise for selling products. It was simply a celebration, a get-together for the faithful to remember the wisdom and teachings of the Great Buddha.

Buddha's Birthday Photographs

A beautiful array of paper lanterns strung across Bongwonsa

Beneath the lanterns are tables with temple offerings and food

Carpets installed for worshipers

A beautiful paper mache representation of a dragon. Note the red lantern above

Sayings of the Buddha in Hangeul (Korean script). Note the red lantern
with the yellow swastika on it- a well-known Buddhist symbol

Age-old representations of the Buddha and boddhisatvas

Offerings of rice on an alter in front of the Buddha

Buddhist revelers dancing and holding picnics (photo 1)

Buddhist revelers dancing and holding picnics (photo 1)

The Way Things Were

Everything that I saw at the Buddhist temples in Seoul happened 16 to 25 years ago. In so many ways my observations are a time capsule of what was. I remember the doors to the temples. Heavy wooden doors hand carved centuries ago with fading paint that defined their age. The open crevices were covered with the finest mulberry paper to keep out the winds and provide insulation for the inside. The wooden floors that had been constructed long ago showing their age as they had been walked upon for centuries by the monks, nuns and priests with their traditional shoes. The Buddha statues sitting serenely in their place of worship as the faded walls and intricately carved ceilings were barely seen in the barely lit buildings. The monks and nuns barely made a sound as they walked by from one temple to the next. The temple grounds were little more than mud and sandy soil common of the mountainous areas that many of these temples were located. The stone steps and dirt ramps that led to the shrines seemed to have changed little from year to year during the years that I had gone to visit these holy places. The old stone lanterns that had been on the grounds of the temple for who knows how long, now covered with moss and dirt, probably had fires lit in them so that monks and nuns could find their way through the paths at night.

Indeed, it seemed that these places had changed hardly at all probably since the late Joseon times (1860 to 1897), the era of the Korean Empire (1897 to 1910) and the early part of the Japanese colonial period (1910 to 1920). Electricity was brought to the temples during the Japanese period so the monks did not have to rely on candles which could cause fire. Beyond this, the temples changed little even as Seoul all around them changed significantly. Above all else, the temples were historical and holy shrines to the teachings of Lord Buddha. The monks, nuns and priests had taken vows of simplicity and of devoting their lives to the teachings of Lord Buddha. They lived the same way as those before them had done. One of the reasons why I went to these temples was to get away from the extreme modernity of Seoul to a more quiet, simpler life. What I saw years back in the time I lived in Seoul was how the adherents of the Buddhist faith had lived as had those who had gone before them 80 to over 100 years before. In so many ways the way of life of these followers of Lord Buddha had followed a more quiet, monastic way of life that had been followed for centuries.

From what my wife's family and friends have informed us, plus recent youtube videos we have seen within recent years, all of this seems to have changed. It seems that these temples are no longer the quiet, spartan places they once were. Theme gardens, fish ponds and more touristy kitsch has been added to attract tourists and bring in revenue. In a way it is disappointing that these changes have taken place, but maybe it was inevitable because of how much Seoul itself had grown and changed as it has become a 21st Century city. I guess there was no way that the Buddhist orders could keep out the modern and futuristic world with all its comforts and problems. I guess that for Buddhism in Seoul to adapt to the ways and attitudes of an ever-changing world it had to adapt to the modern comforts people in the rest of Seoul are used to. I do not condemn what inevitably may have had to be. My photos can only show what I knew; the memories of the places I walked through a long time ago. As those readers who are now seeing these places in the current era, I hope my memories will serve as a reminder of what once was.

Printed in the United States
by Baker & Taylor Publisher Services